A QUICK GUIDE TO
GUITAR CHORDS

Fast, Easy Approach to Simple One, Two, and Three Finger Chords, Plus Dozens of Popular Songs to Get You Started!

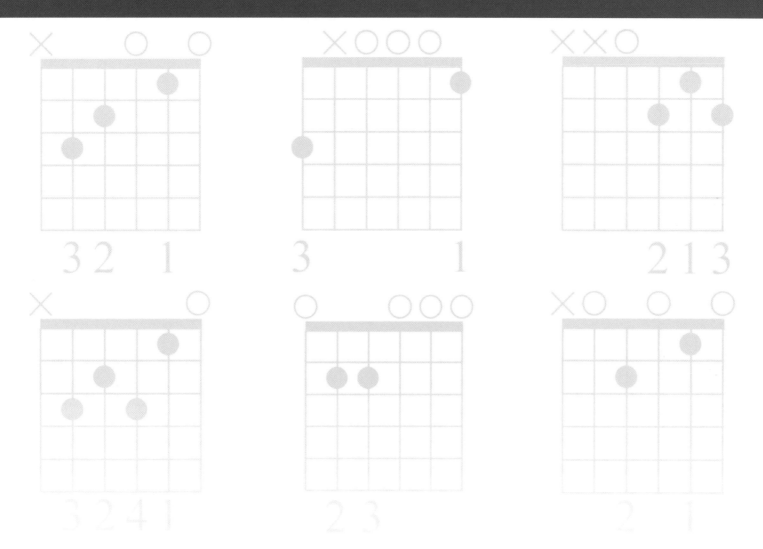

BY STEVE GORENBERG

ISBN 978-1-5400-3569-1

Copyright © 2019 by HAL LEONARD LLC
International Copyright Secured   All Rights Reserved

Visit Hal Leonard Online at
www.halleonard.com

Contact us:
Hal Leonard
7777 West Bluemound Road
Milwaukee, WI 53213
Email: info@halleonard.com

In Europe, contact:
Hal Leonard Europe Limited
42 Wigmore Street
Marylebone, London, W1U 2RN
Email: info@halleonardeurope.com

In Australia, contact:
Hal Leonard Australia Pty. Ltd.
4 Lentara Court
Cheltenham, Victoria, 3192 Australia
Email: info@halleonard.com.au

TABLE OF CONTENTS

INTRODUCTION

Congratulations on your decision to learn how to play guitar! This book is a great introduction to simple guitar chords and songs. If you've never played guitar or any other instrument, *A Quick Guide to Guitar Chords* is an excellent place to begin because it doesn't require you to have any prior musical experience. Many of the examples in this book have been simplified to get you playing immediately, without having to learn how to read traditional music.

This book begins with a quick introduction: how to hold the guitar and how to read chord diagrams—just the very basics to get you started. The next chapter contains chords that only require one finger, plus examples from real songs that you can play right away. From there, we'll progress to simple two-finger chords with accompanying song examples. The chapter after that explores full three-finger chords—the basic guitar chords used to play hundreds of songs in many different styles.

Be patient and take your time in the beginning; once you've learned the basics and can change chords smoothly, you'll be well on your way. The final section of this book contains five complete songs that can be played by using the chords you've learned in the previous chapters. By the time you finish this book, you'll be equipped with all the chords you'll need to continue your musical journey. Grab your guitar and let's get started!

GETTING STARTED

Holding the Pick

Hold the pick in your hand by gripping it firmly between your thumb and first finger. Keep the rest of your hand relaxed and your fingers slightly curved and out of the way. You can strum the strings with a *downstroke* (downward motion) or an *upstroke* (upward motion).

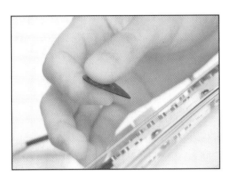

Fret-Hand Position

Keep your hand relaxed and your fingers arched. The first joint of your thumb and your fingertips are the only parts of your hand that should be touching the guitar. Avoid gripping the neck like a baseball bat; your palm should not be touching the guitar neck.

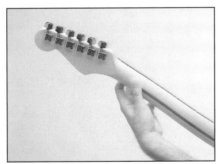

Place the first joint of your thumb on the back of the guitar neck.

Curl your fingers so that only your fingertips are touching the strings.

To indicate chord fingerings, numbers are assigned to the fingers of your fret hand (1 = index, 2 = middle, 3 = ring, 4 = pinky).

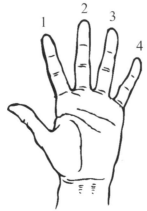

Reading Chord Diagrams

Chords are taught in this book by using graphic representations of the fretboard, or *chord diagrams*. The vertical lines in the diagrams represent the strings; the horizontal lines represent the frets. The thick horizontal line at the top of the diagram represents the nut. Chord diagrams visually correspond to the guitar as if you stood the guitar up from floor to ceiling and looked directly at the fretboard.

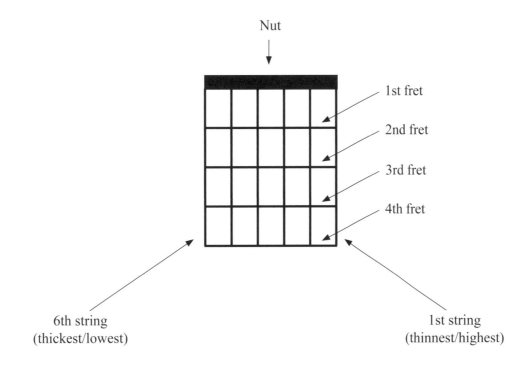

The following symbols are placed on the chord diagrams to show you how to finger the chords:

- The black dots on the diagram indicate which notes are fretted (pressed down) with fingers.

- The fingers used to fret each note are shown underneath the chord diagram.

- The "O" above the diagrams indicate which strings are strummed open (with no fingers touching them).

- An "X" above the diagram indicates that the string should be muted or not strummed.

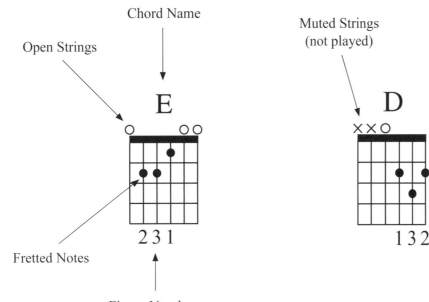

ONE-FINGER CHORDS

Let's get started with some simple chords that only require one finger. The chords in this chapter are simplified versions of the full, open chords that we'll get to later on. For now, these will get you started so you can play some songs right away.

When fretting a note, press down firmly with just your fingertip; be careful not to touch any of the other surrounding strings and accidentally mute them. Strum only the strings that are required, as indicated in the chord diagrams. To confirm that you're fretting the notes properly, pick each string individually to hear if they're ringing out cleanly.

C and G Chords

For the C chord, fret the note on the second string with your first finger and strum only the highest three strings. For the G chord, fret the note on the first string with your third finger and strum only the highest four strings.

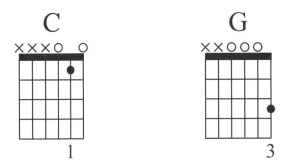

Practice changing from chord to chord in a smooth, even motion to prepare you for playing songs.

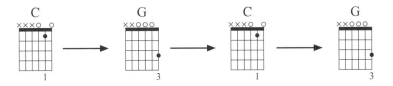

In the example below, strum each chord four times in a downward motion before changing to the next one. Count along in time and change chords without a pause or hesitation at the beginning of each measure.

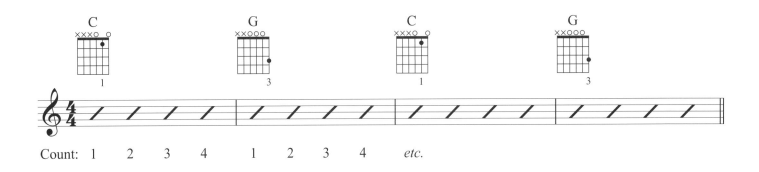

ABC – The Jackson 5

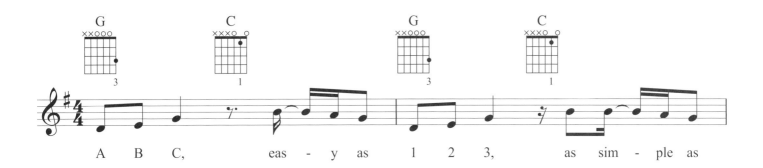

A B C, eas - y as 1 2 3, as sim - ple as

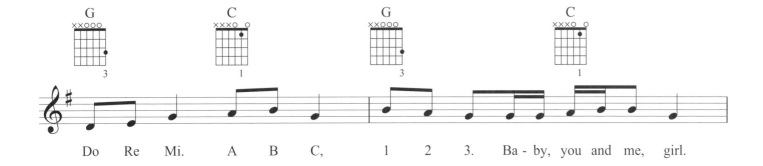

Do Re Mi. A B C, 1 2 3. Ba - by, you and me, girl.

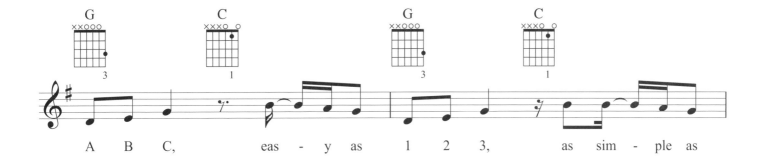

A B C, eas - y as 1 2 3, as sim - ple as

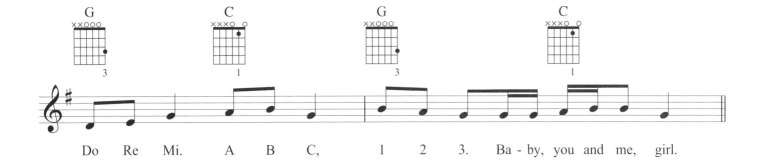

Do Re Mi. A B C, 1 2 3. Ba - by, you and me, girl.

Words and Music by Alphonso Mizell, Frederick Perren, Deke Richards and Berry Gordy
Copyright © 1970 Jobete Music Co., Inc.
Copyright Renewed
All Rights Administered by Sony/ATV Music Publishing LLC, 424 Church Street, Suite 1200, Nashville, TN 37219
International Copyright Secured   All Rights Reserved

G7 Chord

To play a G7 chord, fret the note on the first string with your first finger and strum only the highest four strings.

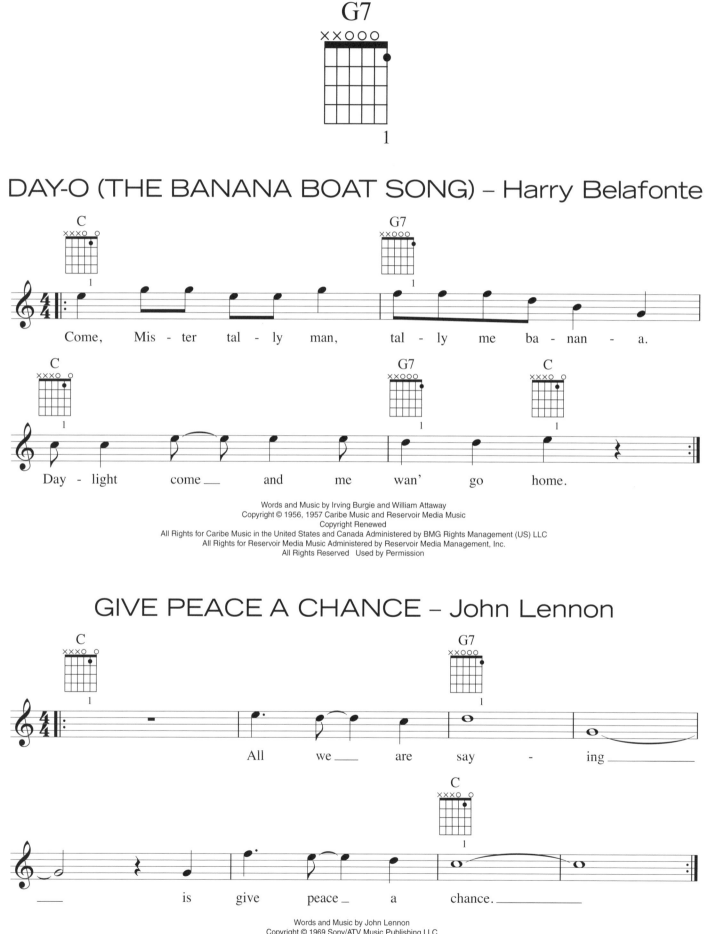

DAY-O (THE BANANA BOAT SONG) – Harry Belafonte

Come, Mis - ter tal - ly man, tal - ly me ba - nan - a.

Day - light come ___ and me wan' go home.

GIVE PEACE A CHANCE – John Lennon

All we ___ are say - ing ___

___ is give peace ___ a chance. ___

Em Chord

To play the E minor chord (written as "Em"), fret the note on the fourth string with your second finger; strum only the highest four strings.

ELEANOR RIGBY – The Beatles

Ah, _____ look at all _____ the lone - ly peo - ple! _____

SOMETHING IN THE WAY – Nirvana

Some - thing in the way. _____ Mm. _____

Some - thing in the way, _____ yeah. Mm. _____

TWO-FINGER CHORDS

In this chapter, we'll take a look at some simple chords that can be fretted with two fingers and combine them with the previous one-finger chords to play some popular songs.

Am and F Chords

Simple versions of the Am and F chords can be played on the highest three strings. Both require two fingers, but the F chord contains a *barre*—using one finger to press down multiple strings at a particular fret. For the F chord, lay your first finger flat across strings 1 and 2 at the first fret. In the chord diagram, the barre is indicated by a curved line, or *slur*, connecting the two dots.

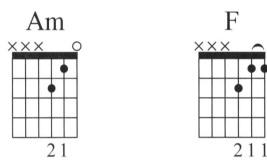

WHAT'S UP – 4 Non Blondes

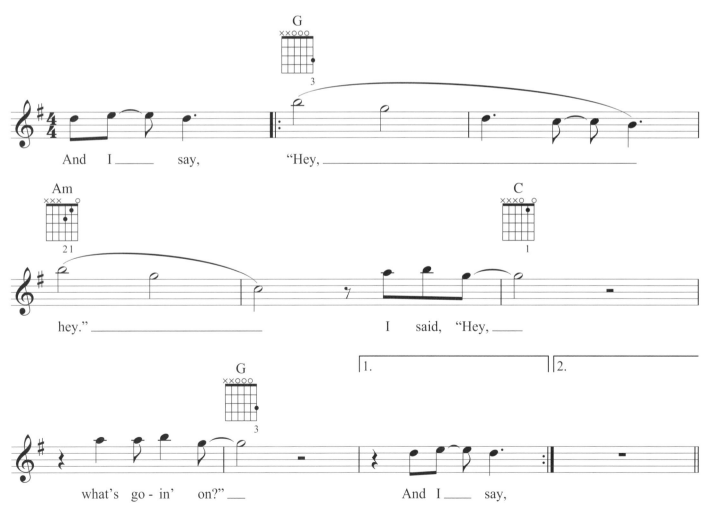

Words and Music by Linda Perry
Copyright © 1992 Sony/ATV Music Publishing LLC and Stuck In The Throat Music
All Rights Administered by Sony/ATV Music Publishing LLC, 424 Church Street, Suite 1200, Nashville, TN 37219
International Copyright Secured All Rights Reserved

ALL THE SMALL THINGS – Blink-182

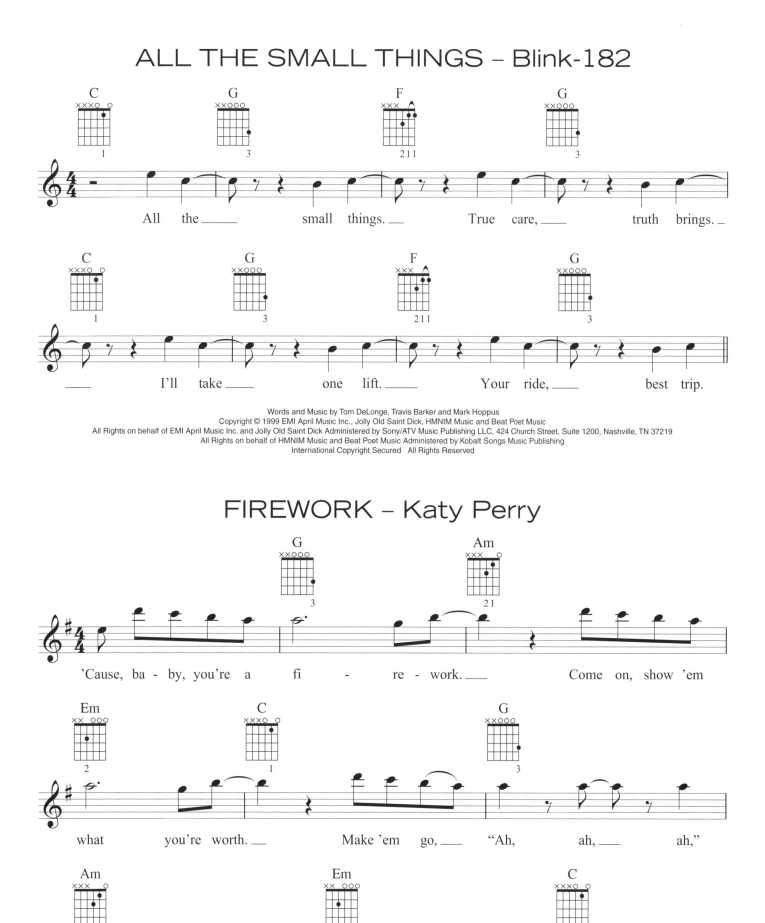

All the ____ small things. __ True care, ___ truth brings. __

__ I'll take ___ one lift. __ Your ride, ___ best trip.

FIREWORK – Katy Perry

'Cause, ba - by, you're a fi - re - work. __ Come on, show 'em

what you're worth. __ Make 'em go, __ "Ah, ah, __ ah,"

as you shoot a - cross the sky - y - y.

PHOTOGRAPH – Ed Sheeran

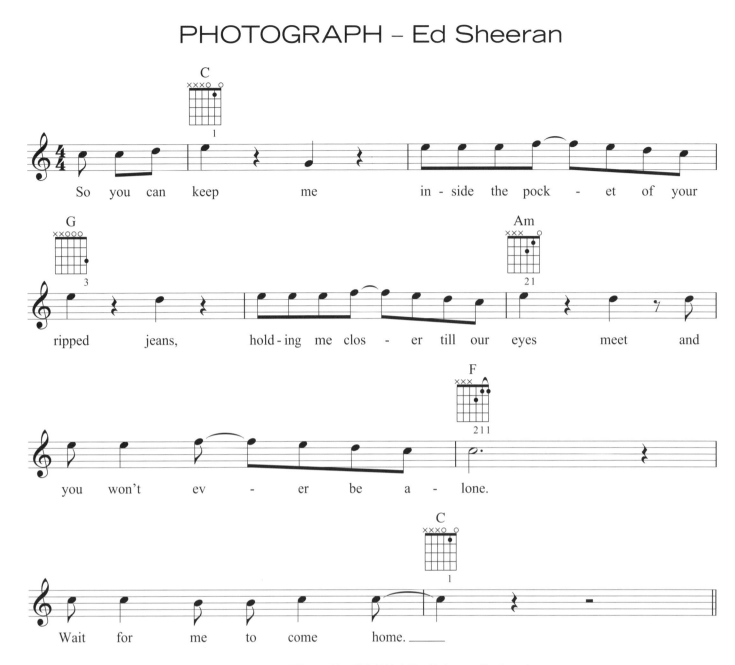

So you can keep me in - side the pock - et of your
ripped jeans, hold - ing me clos - er till our eyes meet and
you won't ev - er be a - lone.
Wait for me to come home. _____

Words and Music by Ed Sheeran, Johnny McDaid, Martin Peter Harrington and Tom Leonard
Copyright © 2014 Sony/ATV Music Publishing (UK) Limited, Spirit B-Unique Polar Patrol, Halosongs and Halomani Songs/Softgrass Songs
All Rights on behalf of Sony/ATV Music Publishing (UK) Limited Administered by Sony/ATV Music Publishing LLC, 424 Church Street, Suite 1200, Nashville, TN 37219
All Rights on behalf of Spirit B-Unique Polar Patrol Administered by Spirit B-Unique Polar Patrol Songs
All Rights on behalf of Halosongs and Halomani Songs/Softgrass Songs Administered by Concord Copyrights and Concord Sounds
International Copyright Secured   All Rights Reserved

E, A, and D Chords

Here are simple two-finger versions of the E, A, and D chords. For the E chord, strum the highest four strings.
For the A chord, strum the highest three strings. For the D chord, strum only the highest two strings.

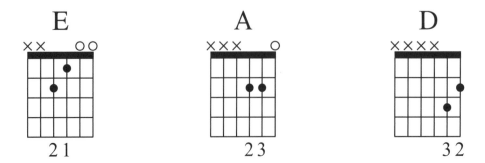

JOHNNY B. GOODE – Chuck Berry

Go! Go! ___ Go, ___ John-ny! Go! Go! ___ Go, ___

___ John-ny! Go! Go! ___ Go, ___ John-ny! Go! Go! ___ Go, ___

___ John-ny! Go! Go! ___ John-ny B. Goode. _

WILD THING – The Troggs

Wild thing, you make my heart sing. You make ev -

- 'ry-thing groov-y. ___ Wild thing.

THREE-FINGER CHORDS

Now that you've learned how to change from chord to chord by using the simplified versions in the previous chapters, it's time to move on to the full, three-finger open chords. The chords in this chapter are the standard open chords used in many songs in the rest of this book.

A, G, D, and E Chords

Here are the full A, G, D, and E chords. For the A chord, strum only the highest five strings; for the D chord, strum only the highest four strings. The G and E chords use all six strings. As in the previous chapters, practice transitioning smoothly from chord to chord without pausing.

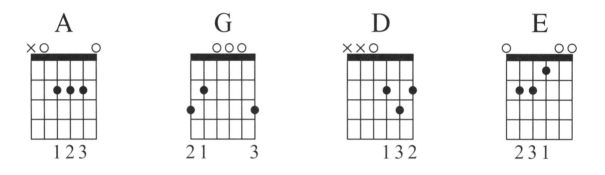

JANE SAYS – Jane's Addiction

Words and Music by Perry Farrell, Dave Navarro, Stephen Perkins and Eric Avery
Copyright © 1988 I'LL HIT YOU BACK MUSIC, EMBRYOTIC MUSIC, SWIZZLESTICK MUSIC and BUBBLY ORANGE STUFF MUSIC
All Rights for I'LL HIT YOU BACK MUSIC, EMBRYOTIC MUSIC and SWIZZLESTICK MUSIC Administered by IRVING MUSIC, INC.
All Rights for BUBBLY ORANGE STUFF MUSIC Administered by SONY/ATV MUSIC PUBLISHING LLC, 424 Church Street, Suite 1200, Nashville, TN 37219
All Rights Reserved   Used by Permission

She hides ___ her tel - e - vi - sion. ___

Says, "I don't owe ___ him noth - ing." ___

SWEET CAROLINE – Neil Diamond

Sweet Car - o - line, ___ good times nev - er seemed so

good. I've been in - clined ___

to be - lieve ___ they nev - er would...

Words and Music by Neil Diamond
Copyright © 1969 STONEBRIDGE-MUSIC, INC.
Copyright Renewed
All Rights Administered by UNIVERSAL TUNES
All Rights Reserved   Used by Permission

USED TO LOVE HER – Guns N' Roses

I used to love _____ her, but I had to kill ____ her.

I used to love _____ her, mm _____ yeah, but I had to kill ____ her.

I had to put ____ her six feet un - der

and I can still ____ hear her __ com - plain. __

Words and Music by W. Axl Rose, Slash, Izzy Stradlin', Duff McKagan and Steven Adler
Copyright © 1988 Guns N' Roses Music (ASCAP) and Black Frog Music (ASCAP)
All Rights for Black Frog Music in the U.S. and Canada Controlled and Administered by Universal - PolyGram International Publishing, Inc.
International Copyright Secured   All Rights Reserved

Em and C Chords

Here are two popular, full versions of the Em and C chords; these two chords are often used together in chord progressions. Notice that the E minor chord only requires two fingers and all six strings are strummed. For the C chord, only strum the highest five strings.

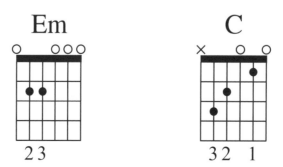

POKER FACE – Lady Gaga

Can't read my, ___ can't read my, ___ no, he can't read ___ my

pok - er face. ___ (She's got me like no-bod - y.)

IN THE END – Linkin Park

I tried so hard ___ and got so ___ far, ___ but in the end, ___

___ it does-n't e - ven mat - ter. I had to fall ___ to lose it ___ all, ___

___ but in the end, ___ it does-n't e - ven mat - ter. ___

Am, F, and Dm Chords

Here are the full versions of the Am, F, and Dm chords. Strum only the highest five strings for the Am chord; for the other two chords, strum only the highest four strings. The F chord will probably be the most challenging for you since it includes the barre and also requires you to stretch your third finger up to the third fret to voice the note on the fourth string.

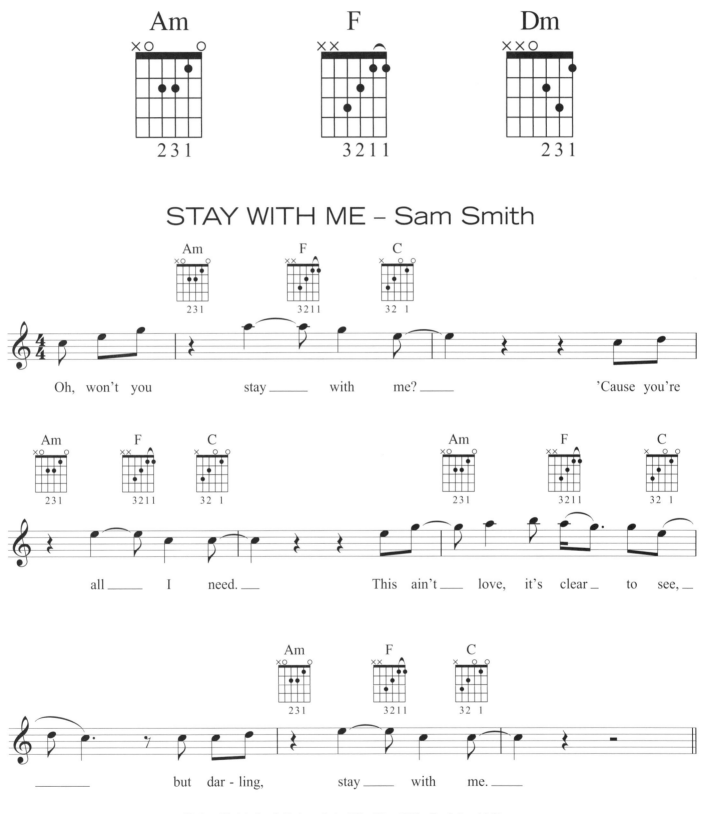

TRY – Pink

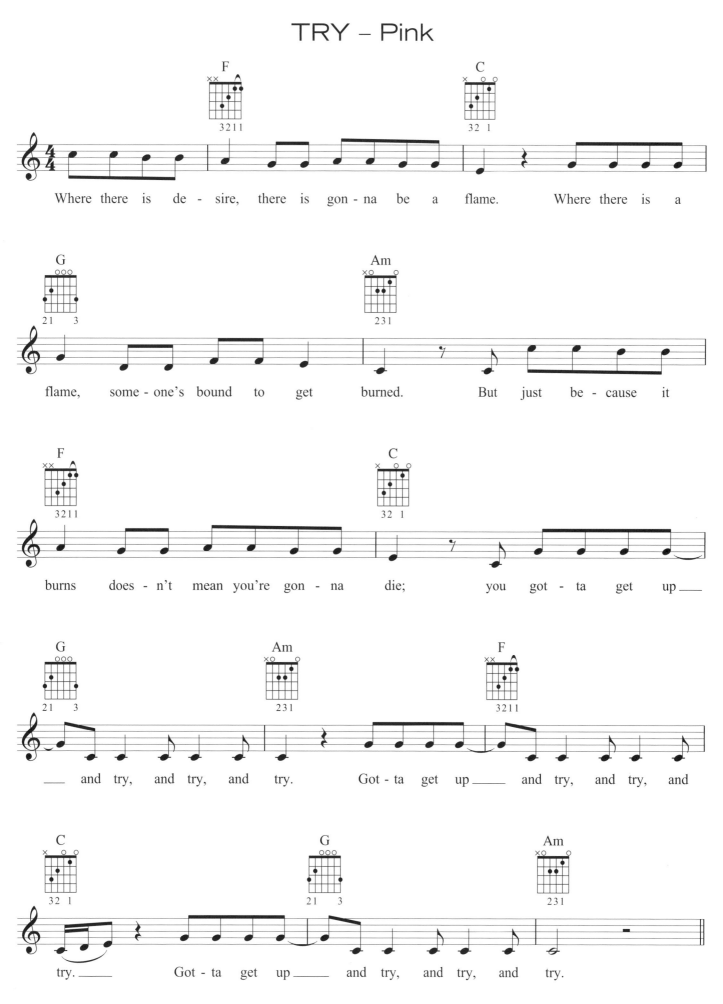

Words and Music by busbee and Ben West
Copyright © 2010 BMG Platinum Songs, Hello I Love You Music and Legitimate Efforts Music
All Rights Administered by BMG Rights Management (US) LLC

AIN'T NO SUNSHINE – Bill Withers

Ain't no sun - shine when she's gone.

It's not warm __ when she's a - way.

Ain't no sun - shine when she's gone, __ and she's al - ways gone too

long an - y - time __ she goes a - way.

Words and Music by Bill Withers
Copyright © 1971 INTERIOR MUSIC CORP.
Copyright Renewed
All Rights Controlled and Administered by SONGS OF UNIVERSAL, INC.
All Rights Reserved   Used by Permission

GET LUCKY – Daft Punk

She's up __ all night __ till the sun, I'm up __ all night __ to get some.

She's up __ all night __ for good fun, I'm up __ all night __ to get luck - y.

Words and Music by Thomas Bangalter, Guy Manuel Homem Christo, Nile Rodgers and Pharrell Williams
Copyright © 2013 Concord Copyrights, XLC Music, EMI April Music Inc. and More Water From Nazareth
All Rights for Concord Copyrights Administered by Concord Music Publishing
All Rights for XLC Music, EMI April Music Inc. and More Water From Nazareth Administered by Sony/ATV Music Publishing LLC, 424 Church Street, Suite 1200, Nashville, TN 37219
All Rights Reserved   Used by Permission

ADVANCED CHORDS

In this chapter, we'll explore some popular and useful advanced chords. Some require all four fingers to fret the notes. These will be a little more challenging, especially when changing chords.

Dsus4, Dsus2, and D7 Chords

The Dsus4 and Dsus2 chords are often used in combination with the regular D chord. While fretting and holding the regular D chord shape, simply add your fourth finger to play the sus4 version; lift your second finger to play the sus2 version. The D7 chord is also a useful addition to your repertoire.

FREE FALLIN' – Tom Petty

And I'm free,   free

fall - in'.   Yeah, I'm   free,

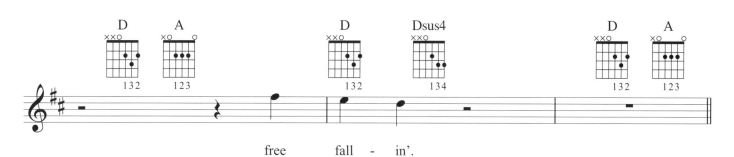

free   fall - in'.

Words and Music by Tom Petty and Jeff Lynne
Copyright © 1989 Gone Gator Music and EMI April Music Inc.
All Rights for EMI April Music Inc. Administered by Sony/ATV Music Publishing LLC, 424 Church Street, Suite 1200, Nashville, TN 37219
All Rights Reserved   Used by Permission

HEY JUDE – The Beatles

Words and Music by John Lennon and Paul McCartney
Copyright © 1968 Sony/ATV Music Publishing LLC
Copyright Renewed
All Rights Administered by Sony/ATV Music Publishing LLC, 424 Church Street, Suite 1200, Nashville, TN 37219
International Copyright Secured   All Rights Reserved

A7, B7, B, and Bm Chords

Here are some more commonly used advanced chords. The B7, B, and Bm chords all require four fingers to fret the notes.

GIVE A LITTLE BIT – Supertramp

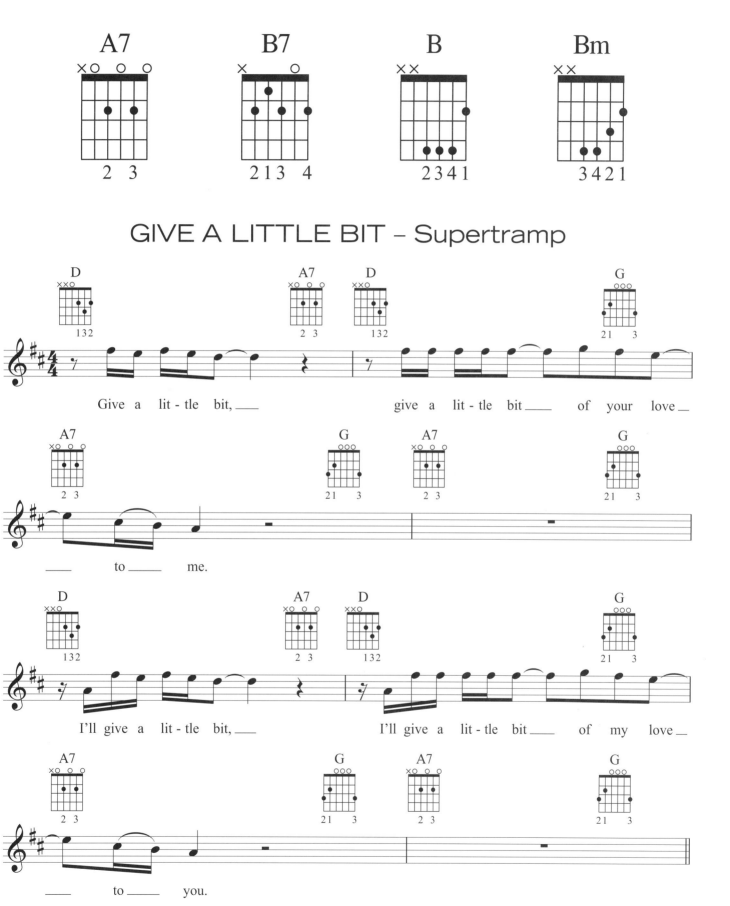

Give a lit - tle bit, ___ give a lit - tle bit ___ of your love ___ ___ to ___ me.

I'll give a lit - tle bit, ___ I'll give a lit - tle bit ___ of my love ___ ___ to ___ you.

Words and Music by Rick Davies and Roger Hodgson
Copyright © 1977 ALMO MUSIC CORP. and DELICATE MUSIC
Copyright Renewed
All Rights Controlled and Administered by ALMO MUSIC CORP.
All Rights Reserved   Used by Permission

HOTEL CALIFORNIA – The Eagles

Words and Music by Don Henley, Glenn Frey and Don Felder
© 1976, 1977 (Renewed) CASS COUNTY MUSIC, RED CLOUD MUSIC and FINGERS MUSIC
All Rights for CASS COUNTY MUSIC Administered by SONGS OF UNIVERSAL, INC.
All Print Rights for CASS COUNTY MUSIC and RED CLOUD MUSIC Administered by WARNER-TAMERLANE PUBLISHING CORP.
All Rights for FINGERS MUSIC Administered by 2850 MUSIC
All Rights Reserved   Used by Permission

I'M GONNA BE (500 MILES) – The Proclaimers

But I would walk five hun-dred miles and I would walk five hun-dred more just to

be the man who walked a thou-sand miles to fall down at your door. __

WRECKING BALL – Miley Cyrus

I came in like a wreck - ing ball. I nev - er hit so

hard in love. All I want-ed was to break your walls. All you ev - er did was __

break __ me. Yeah, you, you wreck __ me.

You've probably noticed that the B and Bm chords contain no open strings; all of the notes in both chords are fretted. Chords with no open strings are referred to as "closed-position" chords, which makes them moveable; that is, they can be transposed simply by moving them to a different fret. For example, you can move the B and Bm chords down one fret to play the B♭ and B♭m chords.

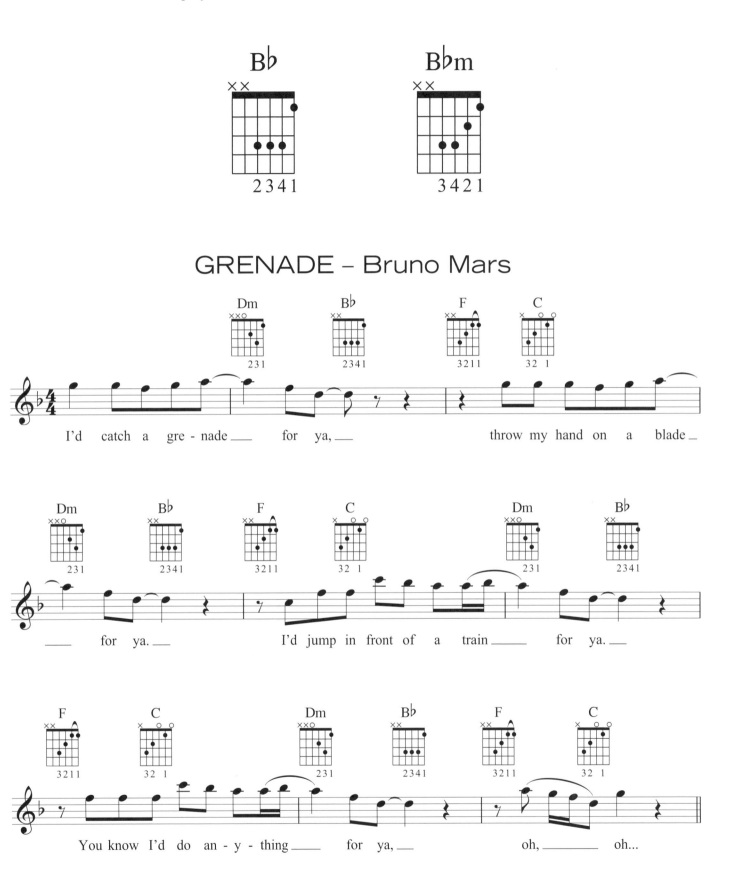

GRENADE – Bruno Mars

I'd catch a gre-nade ___ for ya, ___ throw my hand on a blade ___

___ for ya. ___ I'd jump in front of a train ___ for ya. ___

You know I'd do an-y-thing ___ for ya, ___ oh, ___ oh...

GOOD RIDDANCE
(TIME OF YOUR LIFE)

Words by Billie Joe
Music by Green Day

It's not a ques - tion, but __ a les - son __ learned __ in ___
For what it's worth, __ it ___ was worth _____ all _____ the __

Chorus

time. }
while. }
It's some - thing un - pre - dict - a - ble, ___ but

in the end ___ is right. ___ I hope you had ___ the time _

_____ of ___ your life. ___

1., 2.

It's some-thing un — pre-dict — a — ble, ___ but in the end ___ is right. ___ I hope you had ___ the time ___ ___ of ___ your life. ___

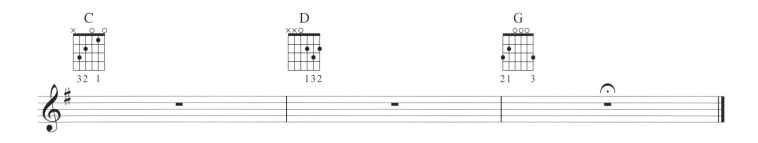

PATIENCE

Words and Music by W. Axl Rose, Slash, Izzy Stradlin',
Duff McKagan and Steven Adler

Was a time when I was-n't sure, _ but you set my mind _ at ease. _

____ There is no doubt ____ you're in ____ my heart ____

_____ now.

Chorus

Said, "Wom-an, take it slow, _ it-'ll work it-self ___ out fine. _

____ All we need ___ is just a lit-tle pa-

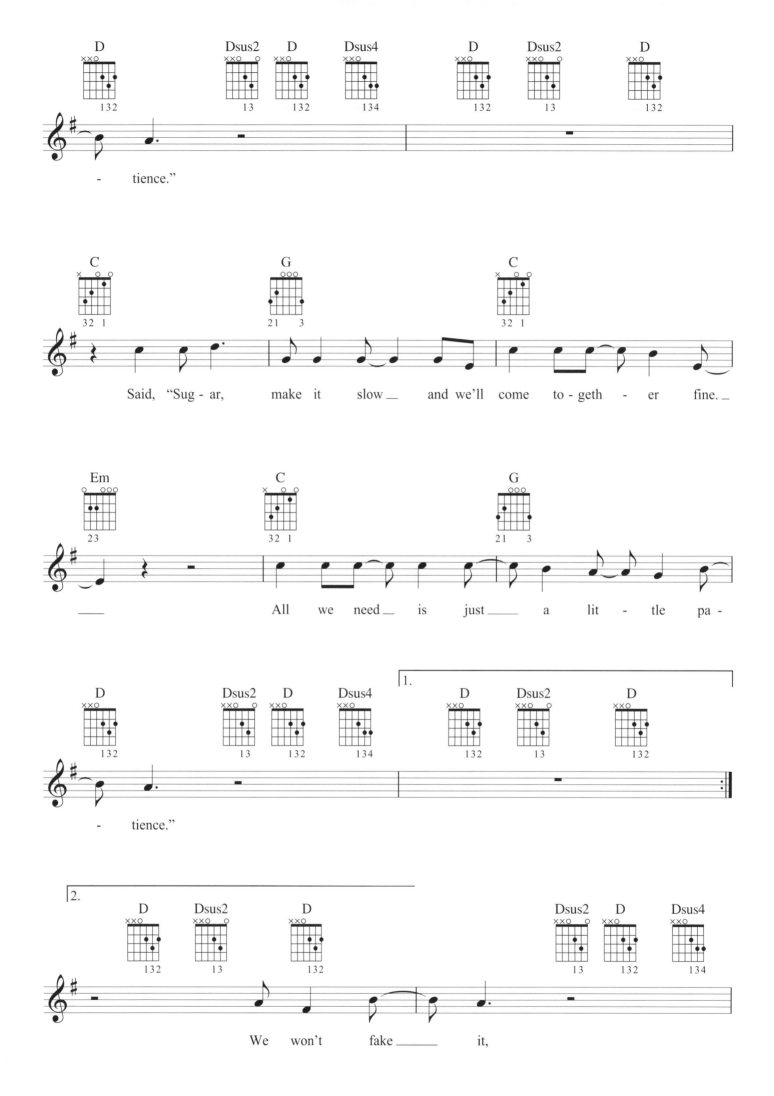

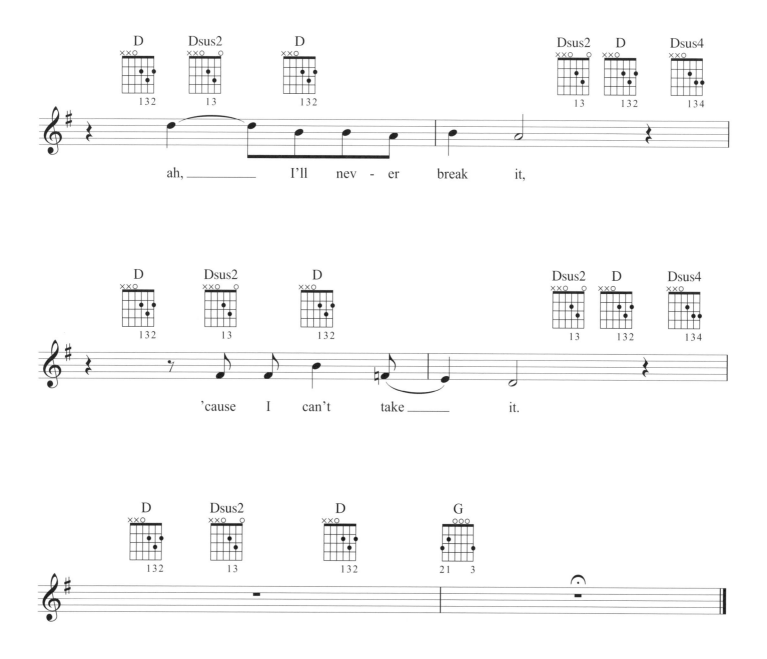

ah, _____ I'll nev - er break it,

'cause I can't take _____ it.

Additional Lyrics

2. I sit here on the stairs 'cause I'd rather be alone.
   If I can't have you right now, I'll wait, dear.
   Sometimes I get so tense, but I can't speed up the time.
   But you know, love, there's one more thing to consider.

Chorus: Said, "Woman, take it slow, and things will be just fine.
   You and I'll just use a little patience."
   Said, "Sugar, take the time 'cause the lights are shining bright.
   You and I've got what it takes to make it."
   We won't fake it, ah, I'll never break it, 'cause I can't take it.

MILLION REASONS

Words and Music by Stefani Germanotta, Mark Ronson and Hillary Lindsey

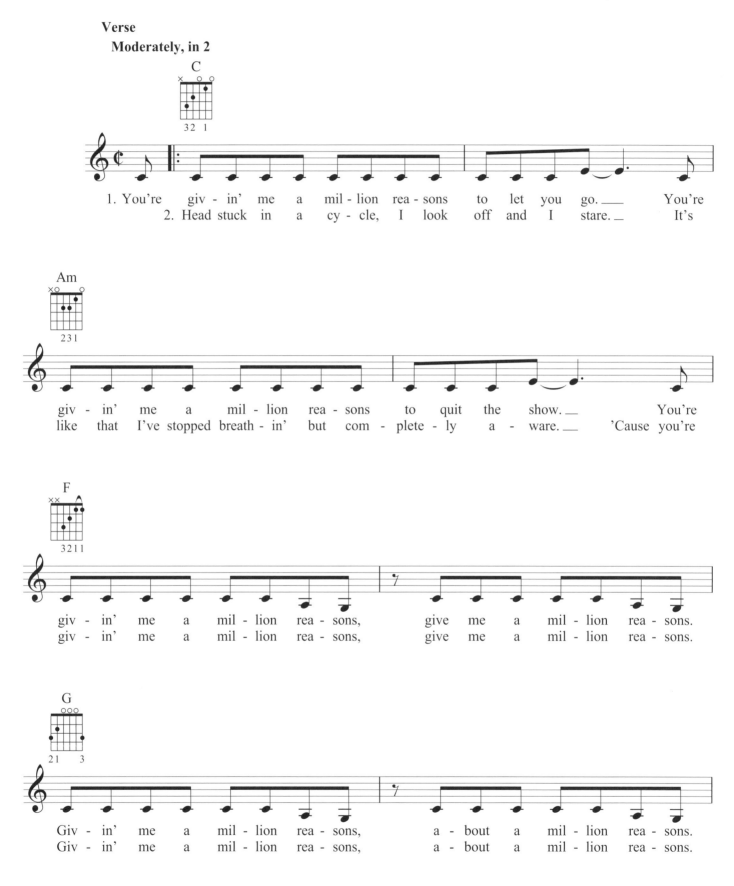

Verse

Moderately, in 2

C

1. You're giv- in' me a mil - lion rea - sons to let you go. ___ You're
2. Head stuck in a cy - cle, I look off and I stare. _ It's

Am

giv - in' me a mil - lion rea - sons to quit the show. ___ You're
like that I've stopped breath - in' but com - plete - ly a - ware. __ 'Cause you're

F

giv - in' me a mil - lion rea - sons, give me a mil - lion rea - sons.
giv - in' me a mil - lion rea - sons, give me a mil - lion rea - sons.

G

Giv - in' me a mil - lion rea - sons, a - bout a mil - lion rea - sons.
Giv - in' me a mil - lion rea - sons, a - bout a mil - lion rea - sons.

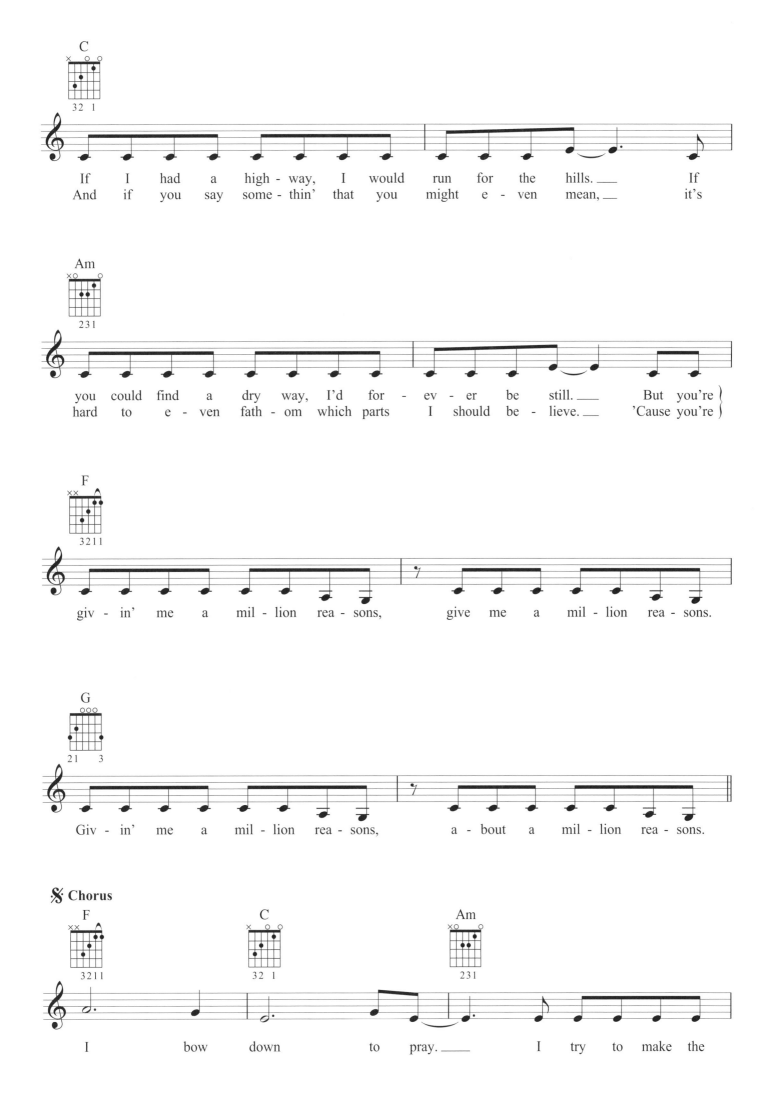

If I had a high-way, I would run for the hills. ___ If
And if you say some-thin' that you might e-ven mean, ___ it's

you could find a dry way, I'd for-ev-er be still. ___ But you're
hard to e-ven fath-om which parts I should be-lieve. ___ 'Cause you're

giv-in' me a mil-lion rea-sons, give me a mil-lion rea-sons.

Giv-in' me a mil-lion rea-sons, a-bout a mil-lion rea-sons.

Chorus

I bow down to pray. ___ I try to make the

35

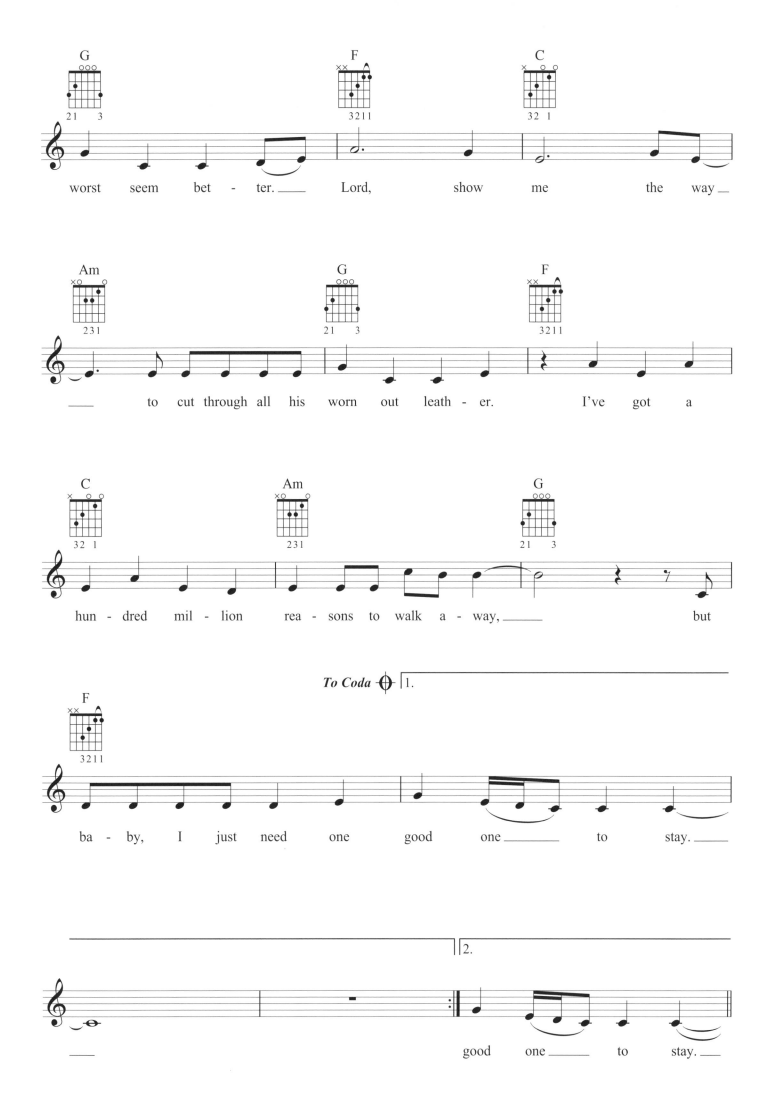

worst seem bet - ter. ___ Lord, show me the way ___

___ to cut through all his worn out leath - er. I've got a

hun - dred mil - lion rea - sons to walk a - way, ___ but

To Coda ⊕ | 1.

ba - by, I just need one good one ___ to stay. ___

| 2.

___ good one ___ to stay. ___

Bridge

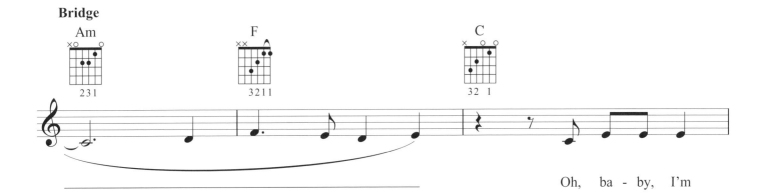

Oh, ba - by, I'm

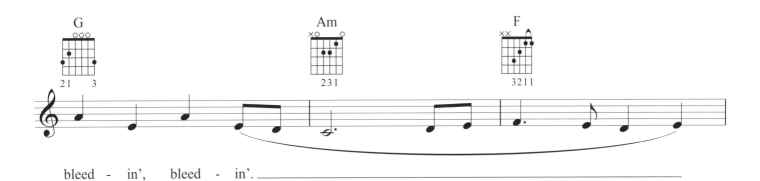

bleed - in', bleed - in'. ____

Can't you give me what I'm need - in', need - in'?

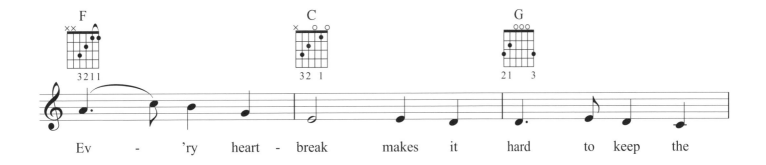

Ev - 'ry heart - break makes it hard to keep the

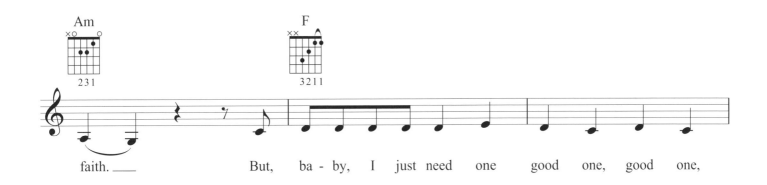

faith. ____ But, ba - by, I just need one good one, good one,

good one, good one, good one, good one. When

Coda

good one, good one. Tell me that you'll be the

good one, good one. Ba - by, I just need one good one — to

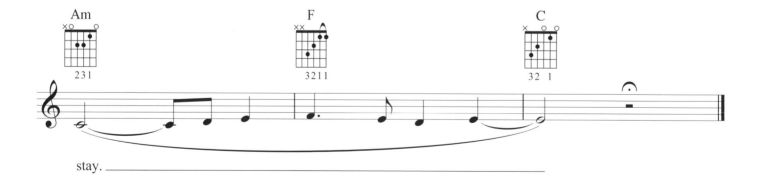

Am   F   C

stay.

LOVE STORY

Words and Music by Taylor Swift

I'll be wait - ing. All there's left to do is run. You'll be the prince and
I keep wait - ing for you, but you nev - er come. Is this in my head? I don't

To Coda ⊕

I'll be the prin - cess. It's a love sto - ry.___ Ba - by, just say___ yes."
know what to think." He knelt to the ground___ and___ pulled out a ring and said,

3. So, "Ro - me - o, save me. They're

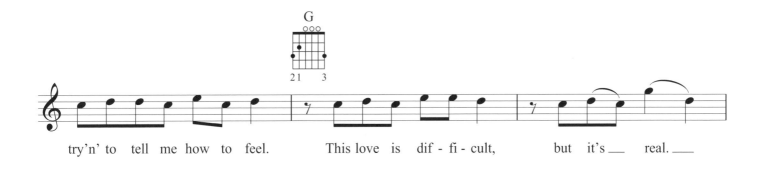

try'n' to tell me how to feel. This love is dif - fi - cult, but it's___ real.___

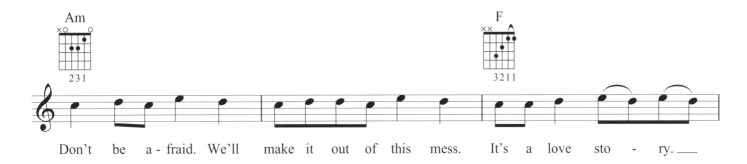

Don't be a - fraid. We'll make it out of this mess. It's a love sto - ry.___

Interlude

Ba - by, just say __ yes."

Bridge

I got tired of wait - ing, __ won - der - in' if

you were ev - er com - ing a - round. __ My faith in you was fad - ing __

D.S. al Coda

__ when I met you on the out - skirts of town. 3. And I said,

Coda

"Mar - ry me, Ju - li - et; you nev - er have to be a - lone.

I love you __ and that's all I real - ly know. I talked to your dad. Go

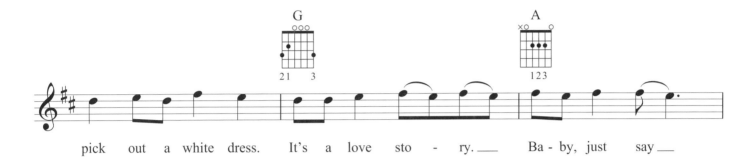

pick out a white dress. It's a love sto - ry. __ Ba - by, just say __

yes." __ Oh, oh, oh, _____

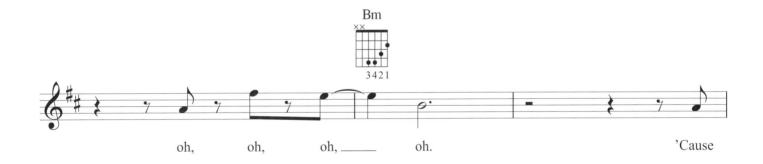

oh, oh, oh, __ oh. 'Cause

we were both young when I first saw __ you. __

NOTHING ELSE MATTERS

Words and Music by James Hetfield and Lars Ulrich

1., 4. So close no mat-ter how far.
2. Nev-er o-pened my-self this way.
3. Trust I seek and I find in you.

Could-n't be much more from the heart.
Life is ours, we live it our way.
Ev-'ry day for us some-thing new.

For-ev-er trust-ing who we are.
All these words I don't just say.
O-pen mind for a dif-f'rent view.

And noth-ing else mat-ters.

Nev - er cared   for what   they   do. _____

Nev - er   cared   for   what   they   know, _____

oh,   but   I   know. _____

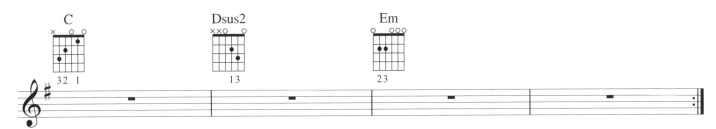

Verse

5. I nev - er o - pened my - self this way. ____
6. Trust I seek and I find in you. ____

Life is ours; we live it our way. ____
Ev - 'ry day for us some - thing new. ____

All these words I don't just say. ____
O - pen mind for a dif - f'rent view. ____

And noth - ing else mat - ters. ____
And noth - ing else mat - ters. ____

Chorus

Nev - er cared for what they say. _____

Nev - er cared for games they play. _____

Nev - er cared for what they do. _____

Nev - er cared for what they know, _____

oh, and I know. _____ Yeah, yeah. _____

Verse

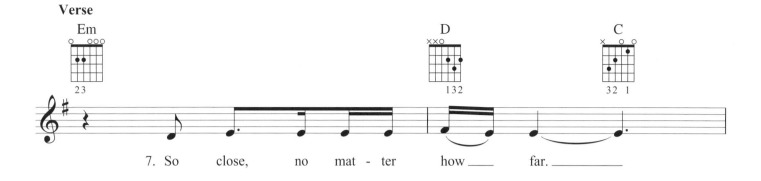

7. So close, no mat - ter how ___ far. _____

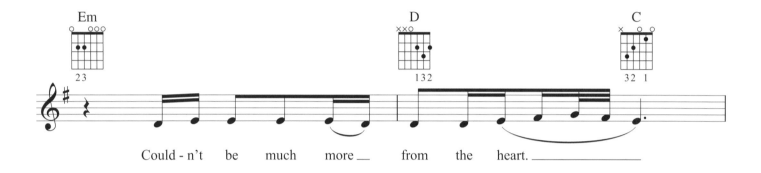

Could - n't be much more ___ from the heart. _____

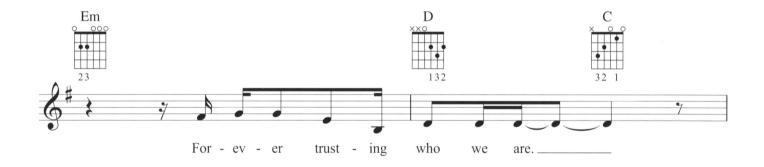

For - ev - er trust - ing who we are. _____

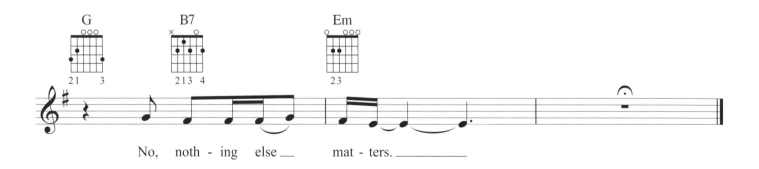

No, noth - ing else ___ mat - ters. _____